THE DESERT TORTOISE

BY SUE FOX

Two Mountain Press
Jackson Hole Wyoming

A portion of the proceeds from the sale of this book will benefit
land preservation efforts by the Nature Conservancy in the Mojave Desert.

For more information:
Tortoise Group
157 Poncho Circle
Las Vegas, NV 89119
Email: tortoisegroup@worldnet.att.net
Website: <tortoisegroup.org>

Photo Credits
Cover: Aaron Mayes/Las Vegas Sun; United States Fish and Wildlife Service: pages 16, 24, 35, 42, 46, 47, 50; Kit Miller: pages 2, 41, 46, 49, back cover; Jennifer Hallett: page 3; Catherine Schmid-Maybach: pages 4, 9, 37, 47; Jim Moore: pages 1, 5, 11, 13, 17, 39, 45, 48, 50; Phil Medica: pages 6, 10, 14, 15, 18-21, 30, 32, 33, 36, 38, 43; Todd Esque: pages 12, 22, 23, 26, 28; Teri Knight: page 34; Karen Kinsella; page 40; all other photos by the author

Acknowledgments
The author thanks the following people for sharing their expertise on desert tortoises and reviewing the manuscript: Phil Medica (US Fish and Wildlife Service), Jim Moore (Nature Conservancy), Betty Burge (Tortoise Group), and Brad Hardenbrook (NV Division of Wildlife), and gives special thanks to my editor, Judy Eddy. Any errors are solely the responsibility of the author.

All rights reserved. No part of this book may be reproduced or transmitted in any form or by any means, electronic or mechanical, including photocopying, recording, scanning, or by any information storage and retrieval system, without written permission from the publisher, except in the case of brief excerpts for review.

Two Mountain Press
PO Box 11822
Jackson WY 83002

Copyright Two Mountain Press (C) 2002

ISBN 0-9679550-1-7

Printed in the United States of America

THE DESERT TORTOISE
BY SUE FOX

Two Mountain Press
Jackson Hole Wyoming

Desert tortoises live in the deserts of the American southwest

A MOVING ROCK

When early settlers traveled through the American deserts, they were often fooled by optical illusions called mirages. The mirages formed visions of shiny blue lakes that faded and disappeared as the thirsty people and their wagon trains got closer. The early travelers might also have been fooled by the sight of a rock slowly moving across the desert. But this rock was not a mirage; it was a desert tortoise.

The tortoise slowly lumbers across the flat desert. Its wrinkly gray skin is lined with dirt from digging. The tortoise keeps its dome-shaped shell high above the ground as it walks. Its hind legs are thick and round and look like elephants' feet. The tortoise has a small head and alert gold-green eyes.

When threatened or frightened, the tortoise withdraws into its shell

Something startles the tortoise and it instantly stops moving. Letting its breath out with a hissing sigh, it quickly pulls its head into the safety of its shell. Then it drops to the ground and draws in its huge shovel-shaped front legs. Like an armored door, its scaly elbows touch, and completely block the shell's opening. It even tucks its tiny tail into the back of its shell. The gentle tortoise waits, relying on its natural armor to protect it from danger.

After a while, the tortoise slowly pulls its head out of its shell and looks around. The danger has passed. It stands up on its legs, raising its shell off the ground, and slowly ambles away. The tortoise pauses to take a bite from a bunch of grass, and then it disappears into the shade of a creosote bush for a midday nap.

The eastern box turtle and red-eared slider are two well known species because they are commonly sold as pets

TYPES OF TURTLES

Tortoises are one of the oldest living types of **reptiles**. Reptiles have scaly skin and lay eggs with a tough outer shell. Lizards, snakes and crocodiles are also reptiles.

More than 25 million years ago, turtles and tortoises roamed through steamy swamps and forests and swam in the oceans with the dinosaurs. Like the giant dinosaurs, some ancient turtles were enormous, more than twenty feet long!

Modern tortoises look similar to the prehistoric ones found in fossils. Fossils show that even ancient turtles had well developed shells. After the dinosaurs became **extinct**, turtles and tortoises still survived.

From dry deserts to the salty ocean, to freshwater ponds and forests, turtles and tortoises have adapted to many different environments. Approximately 250 **species**, or kinds, of tortoises and turtles live on earth today. **Terrestrial** species that live on land are called tortoises. They usually have large shells and big feet. Most tortoises cannot swim well. **Aquatic** species live most or all of their lives in water and are called turtles. They have webbed feet and streamlined shells. All aquatic turtles, even sea turtles, must come ashore to lay their eggs.

An adult tortoise's shell is like a suit of armor

SUIT OF ARMOR

Scientists think that tortoises and turtles survived after the dinosaurs died because of their shell, which covers their backs and bellies like a suit of armor. All tortoises and turtles have some kind of shell. Without their shell, they would die.

Turtle shells come in many shapes and sizes. Some sea turtles, such as the leatherback turtle, have small shells and can swim very fast. The leatherback can grow more than 9 feet (about 3 meters) in length and can weigh almost a ton (907 kilograms).

Not all turtles have hard shells. Softshelled turtles, which live in fresh water, have soft, leathery shells. Using the flexible edges of their shell, they bury themselves in sand or mud. Hidden in shallow water, softshells lie and wait for **prey**, occasionally stretching their long necks to breathe gulps of air with snorkel-like nostrils.

The gigantic tortoises of the Galapagos Islands have shells that look like huge, bony fortresses. These enormous tortoises might have a shell 4 feet (1.2 meters) long and can weigh more than 400 pounds (180 kilograms).

The tortoise's dull color helps camouflage it

Other tortoises have stranger shapes. The pancake tortoise of Africa lives in rocky country. It looks flat because its soft, flexible shell is only about one inch high. When danger threatens, it quickly runs to the closest rocks and squeezes itself into a crevice. Wedged in, the tortoise is almost impossible to pull out. When it is safe again, the tortoise squeezes back out.

A tortoise's shell is made of bone and is very hard. The shell has two parts. The upper part is called the **carapace** and the lower part is called the **plastron**. The two parts are connected at the sides by bony bridges. Just like you, a tortoise has ribs, but they are fused to the inside of its shell. The tortoise's head, chunky legs, and tail poke through openings in the shell. Unlike a hermit crab or what you see in cartoons, turtles and tortoises cannot crawl out of their shells.

The tortoise's shell is made of bony plates that fit together like the seams of clothes. Horny plates, called **scutes**, cover the shell. In some turtles, such as the map turtle, the scutes are marked with beautiful patterns and colors.

Desert tortoises are not colorful. Their shells are various shades of dull brown or gray. Their leathery skin is usually gray or black. Their earthy color helps **camouflage** the tortoises by allowing them to blend in with their surroundings.

Tortoises are famous slowpokes

SLOWPOKES

Tortoises are famous slowpokes. Plodding along, their short legs poking out at the sides, they never seem to be in a hurry. Every step seems to take an effort. Their tough shell is heavy and slows them down, but they do not need to move fast. Carrying a home on one's back is excellent protection. If they feel threatened, they can just hide inside their shell and find a safer place later.

On flat ground, a tortoise can walk about 20 feet (6.2 meters) a minute, or about one fourth of a mile in one hour. (People walk about three miles in one hour.) When it is steep and rocky, tortoises move much slower. Tortoises can seem stubborn. Rather than walk around an object, they often try to climb over whatever is in their way.

However, desert tortoises are not clumsy. They climb up steep **washes** and ravines without tumbling down. They drop off rock shelves and slide through narrow crevices. They even climb into shrubs and cacti to eat flowers and fruit while standing on their hind legs.

The area in blue shows the range of the desert tortoise

LIFE IN THE DESERT

The desert tortoise lives in the Mojave and Sonoran deserts of the southwestern United States. The **range** of the desert tortoise stretches from the southwestern corner of Utah, through the southern tip of Nevada to western Arizona and southeastern California, and south into Mexico.

Deserts are hostile places for animals and plants. The summers are scorching hot and the winters can be freezing cold. In a single day, the temperature can fluctuate by more than 80° F (44.3° C).

In the middle of summer, the desert is quiet except for the hot wind that occasionally rattles the branches of a scrubby bush. Nothing moves except dust devils, miniature tornadoes of dirt and dead plants that spin across the desert and then suddenly disappear.

The summer air is so dry that a piece of bread held in a breeze will become dry and crispy, as if toasted. Clouds can evaporate before your eyes. The blistering heat and drying winds suck moisture out of the desert. Together, they cause more water to be lost through evaporation than falls as rain.

Flowing water from a flash flood created this pattern

The Mojave Desert is the driest part of the United States. Less than 5 inches (12.5 centimeters) of rain falls each year. More than six months can pass without any rain. The plants and animals in the desert must be able to live on very little water. Some deserts have two rainy seasons: winter rains and summer thunderstorms.

Sometimes, so much rain falls during short summer downpours that the dry, baked ground cannot absorb it all. Then the water rushes down washes and gullies, breaking off chunks of dirt and uprooting plants to add to the muddy water. This deluge of water is called a flashflood. It can drown a slow-moving tortoise that is caught unaware in a wash when the water roars through.

The flowers of a Yucca attract moths and other insects

A whole world of strange plants live in the desert. Cacti, plump water-storing plants whose leaves have become thorns, grow in all shapes and sizes. Some cacti look soft and furry, but their "fur" is actually painfully sharp spines and stickers. Other plants are prickly, too. Joshua trees are covered with whorls of sharp, pointed leaves. Their thick, heavy arms bend every which way.

Desert plants have special **adaptations** that help them survive in their environment. Many desert shrubs have small leaves covered with woolly hair or are coated with wax to reduce water loss and reflect the sun's rays. The spindly shrubs grow far apart from each other because they compete for scarce water under the soil surface.

This harsh land is the desert tortoise's **habitat**. In different parts of its range, the tortoise might be found among steep, rocky slopes or it might live in flat desert pavement with washes.

The tortoise's burrow helps it to survive in the desert

THE BURROW

Underneath the slender branches of a creosote bush, a tortoise is digging a burrow. The tortoise uses its powerful front feet and long, strong claws to dig. Its hind feet push the dirt away. When the pile of loosened dirt gets in the way, the tortoise turns around and acts like a bulldozer, shoving the dirt out of the way.

As the hole gets deeper, the tortoise alternates between scooping out dirt and marching in and out of its burrow until it is satisfied with its new home. In less than an hour, the tortoise has dug a burrow that will cover its body. The large pile of dirt at the burrow's entrance is called an apron, which is like the patio of our homes.

Desert tortoises spend most of their time underground in their burrows.

A desert tortoise's burrow is easy to recognize because it is shaped just like the profile of a tortoise. The burrow is flat on the bottom and half-moon shaped on top. The size of a burrow's entrance is similar to the size of the tortoise that dug it. Burrows angle down and usually go straight back. They have one opening and no side branches. Tortoises dig their burrows beneath shrubs, under rocks, in hillsides, or the banks of washes. Sometimes, the tortoises will use natural caves if they are available.

A basking tortoise sprawls on the ground to soak up as much heat as possible

DESERT ADAPTATIONS

As the morning sun rises, a sluggish tortoise crawls out of its burrow. It plops down on the apron of dirt. Sprawled on the ground with its legs and neck extended the tortoise basks in the warm sun. Stretched out, it quickly soaks up the sun's rays. Warmed by the sun, the tortoise can begin its day.

All reptiles, including tortoises, are **ectothermic**. Unlike birds and **mammals**, including you, reptiles cannot make and keep a constant temperature inside their bodies. Their body temperature depends on the temperature of their surroundings. A desert tortoise is active if its body temperature is between 68° to 100° F (20° - 37.7° C).

Tortoises control their body temperature by seeking shade or resting underground during the hottest part of the day

The sun is the tortoise's heater. To raise its body temperature, a tortoise basks in the sun. Some people think that tortoises can tolerate high temperatures because they live in the desert, but this is not true. When the tortoise becomes too warm, it rests under a shady plant. By moving between the sun and shade, a tortoise adjusts its body temperature and stays comfortable. When the desert gets too hot, the tortoise crawls underground into its burrow to cool off and avoid the heat and dry winds.

As the summer days get hotter, tortoises wake up before the sun comes up. They may eat a quick meal and then retreat back underground. Later in the evening, when the sun is lower and the air begins to cool, they might come above the ground again to eat. On hot summer nights, tortoises often sleep outside in **pallets**, which are shallow depressions scratched into the dirt under bushes.

During summer, the desert does not begin to cool until after the scorching sun sets

HOMEBODIES

Desert tortoises spend most of their lives sleeping underground in their burrows. Hidden inside their snug homes, tortoises are protected from the fierce summer heat, drying winds, and freezing winter temperatures on the surface of the desert. Depending on the weather, tortoises might be active above ground for less than three months each year.

Summer burrows slope down to reach the cool soil at the bottom. Some just cover the tortoise's shell, but most are several feet long. They are often temporary and might be used for only one summer. Below the sun-baked ground, the temperature inside a tortoise's burrow stays a relatively cool 75° F (23.8° C), while outside the temperature might be 110° F (43.3° C) or more.

The blazing summer sun can create temperatures of oven-like heat. Day after day, the desert temperatures exceed 100° F (37.7° C). By midafternoon, the temperature on the ground can reach more than 140° F (60° C), hot enough to cook an egg! Because they cannot tolerate such high temperatures, the tortoises **estivate** underground, which means they sleep in their burrow during the driest and hottest part of the year, without eating or drinking for days or weeks.

Naturally occurring caliche caves are used as dens by tortoises

The desert can get cold in the winter. It can even snow! Once the temperature turns cooler in autumn, tortoises move to their deep, winter dens where they stay dry. Winter dens are long, between 4 feet to 36 feet (1.2 meters to 10.9 meters) in length. The temperatures in longer burrows do not fluctuate as much as in the short, summer burrows. During the winter, tortoises sink into a deep sleep called **hibernation**. Their heartbeat and breathing slow down and they survive on stored energy and the water they were able to save during the year.

Sometimes, several tortoises share a winter den. In Utah, 17 tortoises were once found hibernating together. Dens are often under caliche (ke-le-che), a hard, cement-like type of soil that may form natural caves. The caliche dens are used year after year, but not always by the same tortoises. Scientists have found some winter dens in southwestern Utah that might have been in use for 5000 years.

A variety of animals use the burrows dug by desert tortoises, including rattlesnakes

SHARED HOMES

Racing on its tiptoes, a slender whiptail lizard darts into a tortoise burrow and disappears from sight — just in time. The dark shadow of a hunting kestrel glides overhead.

A sidewinder, a type of rattlesnake, left its S-shaped pattern of tracks in the dirt at the entrance of another burrow. Perhaps it is sleeping inside, digesting a mouse after an evening's hunt.

Chased by a galloping roadrunner, a gopher snake quickly slithers down a large tortoise burrow. Following the snake, the roadrunner seizes its victim and takes the snake back outside to eat.

Few plants in the desert provide much shade. Desert animals hide from the sun under rocks and rock piles, in cliffs, in and under bushes, and in underground burrows. The burrows that tortoises dig are important to other animals living in the desert.

Some desert animals do not have long claws and long legs to dig their own burrows so they share the tortoise's underground home. These other animals are called **commensal** species. The tortoises do not harm other creatures who share their burrows, nor are they hurt by them.

A tortoise can spend its entire life within an area of one square mile

A tortoise can spend its entire life in an area less than one square mile in size, called its **home range**. A tortoise's home range overlaps with that of other tortoises. Just as you know your neighborhood and neighbors, a tortoise knows its home range. As it wanders about its home range, a tortoise might dig more burrows. It might even share or switch burrows with a neighbor tortoise. Male tortoises usually have larger home ranges than do females, and large tortoises have larger home ranges than do small tortoises.

Empty tortoise burrows are used by many other animals. Standing on the dirt apron in front of a tortoise burrow, a long-legged burrowing owl suddenly pounces on a beetle walking by. Pairs of burrowing owls move into abandoned tortoise burrows and raise their families. Fluffy feathers and the leftover wings and legs from their insect dinners scattered outside a burrow usually mean that owls are home.

Glossy blackwidow spiders spin their tough webs across old burrows and trap insects seeking shade. Tortoises plow right through the webs when they move back in. Then the spider has to repair its web or find a new place to live.

Summer thunderstorms darken the sky and provide water for desert plants and animals

THE WATER HOLDER

A tortoise's hard shell, leathery skin and thick scales help prevent it from losing water through evaporation. However, tortoises still slowly lose water when they breathe, eat, and walk. You do, too. Blow into your cupped hand. Do you feel the moisture from your breath? For most of the year, tortoises drink little or no water. Tortoises get water from the succulent green plants they eat. But they still need to drink fresh water.

In the hot sun, heat waves shimmer across the desert. It rains only a few inches and a few times each year. The sun and wind cause any rain-filled pools of water to quickly evaporate. Sometimes, sheets of rain hang from clouds but the water never reaches the dusty ground; the dry desert air absorbs it first.

A tortoise drinks rainwater from a depression that it dug

As dark gray clouds grow on the horizon, the sun is hidden from sight. Bolts of lightning brighten the sky and the ground. The boom and rumble of thunder follow each brilliant flash. Summer thunderstorms provide pools of water for the tortoises to drink.

The tortoises can sense when a rainstorm is coming. When the storm sweeps into the desert and drops of rain hit the ground, tortoises gather at catchment basins. These basins fill with water that the tortoises drink. Some tortoises dig shallow basins in the soil before the rain begins and make their own puddles of drinking water.

Looking like spaceships, tortoises gather to drink water on a road after a rainstorm

Tortoises guzzle rainwater. The water is stored in a tortoise's **bladder**, up to one half pint, for future use. Because tortoises recycle their bladder water over and over, they are able to survive more than a year without drinking any more water. Tortoises go months without emptying their bladders. When they are finally able to drink water again, they will urinate to clean out their bladders and drink water to rehydrate themselves.

A tortoise feasts on the flowers and ripe fruit of an Opuntia cactus

THE GRAZER

Tortoises are herbivores and eat only plants. Tender young grasses and flowers are some of their favorite foods. When they find patches of wildflowers, tortoises gorge for days until the plants are all eaten or dried up. They also eat the flowers and juicy red fruit of beavertail cacti.

Every day, tortoises wander from plant to plant, stopping to sniff each one before deciding whether to eat. Using their strong jaws, which have sharp horny edges but no teeth, they take a few bites before continuing on to another plant.

Tortoises graze on fresh green plants when available

Desert annuals are plants that grow quickly after winter rainfalls and live for only a few weeks or months. Other plants, such as shrubs, are perennial, which means they live for many years. The desert is filled with millions of scattered seeds buried in the dirt from these plants. When the winter rain comes, and other conditions such as the temperature, are just right, the seeds sprout and grow.

After a winter with a lot of rain, the desert explodes with colorful wildflowers. A thin carpet of green grass and succulent annual plants grow under and near the shrubs. Tortoises feast and grow faster in a spring following good plant growth than in dry years when fewer seeds sprout and grow.

During droughts, which sometimes last for years, little or no rain falls. The seeds of many desert plants do not sprout but remain buried in the ground waiting for the next rain. Then there is less food for the tortoises. When desert plants are scarce, tortoises must trudge far and wide to find food. If it is too hot, they remain in their burrows until conditions get better.

Bones from dead animals provide valuable sources of calcium for tortoises and other desert animals

TORTOISE TALK

Desert tortoises are solitary animals, but they still have neighbors they "talk" with. Tortoises hiss, grunt and moan but mainly when they are fighting, courting or mating. Tortoises do not have visible ears, but they do have a good sense of hearing. They also sense tiny movements from other animals that make vibrations on the ground.

Tortoises have a keen sense of smell and are always sniffing. As they walk, tortoises sniff the ground. They sniff when they meet each other and when choosing where to dig their burrows. They even use their sense of smell to follow the paths of other tortoises.

A tortoise chases an intruder from his territory

Underneath a tortoise's jaw are two chin glands. These glands are much larger in males than in females. They are important in courtship because the scent they make helps the tortoises tell the male from the female. Tortoises can recognize other tortoises they already know by their chin gland scent.

Tortoises have good eyesight, which they use to find food. The colors they see are similar to those you see, but it appears that they see best the color of flowers and ripe red cactus fruits. Being close to the ground, tortoises have to stretch high up on their legs if they want to see very far.

The two long prongs on a tortoise's shell beneath its neck are called gular horns and are used by males to fight other males and to court females. The male's gular horns are long and curve up, but a female's are short and straight. The male is also larger than the female and has a longer, thicker tail.

These fighting tortoises push with all their might against each other

KING TORTOISE

THUD! With their heads pulled partway into their shells, two male tortoises suddenly rush forward, loudly crashing their shells together. Tortoises do not need antlers, fangs, or claws to fight. They use the gular horns on their shells as battering rams.

When two males first meet, each stretches out its long neck and begins to bob its head up and down. One tortoise usually circles round and round, trying to bite the legs and head of his rival. Then, with their heads pulled into their shells, the two tortoises stand as high as possible to look huge and dangerous. Charging each other, the two males lock their gular horns and have a pushing contest. They push until one tortoise is forced backwards.

The losing tortoise is pushed over onto his back

The fight finally ends when one tortoise turns and hurries away or is flipped over on his back. The loser struggles to turn himself right side up again. Rocking back and forth and spinning around, he twists his front legs and neck to get back on his feet. If the tortoise cannot turn over, he could die, especially during summer.

The male tortoises in a particular area know each other and usually do not waste time and energy fighting. Most of the time, the largest males win the battles so the smaller males avoid them. A smaller, subordinate male shows he does not want to fight by hiding in his shell and lying down or quickly walking away.

Females like the larger males. Because larger males are older, they show that they have good survival abilities, which they might pass on to their offspring.

Courtship and mating occur in spring time

FINDING A PARTNER

With the arrival of warm spring weather, tortoises wake up from their winter sleep. They leave their deep underground burrows and look for plants to eat. If they are old enough, the males look for females to court.

Tortoises do not grow up for a long time. They are not ready to breed until they are 15 to 20 years old, or about seven inches long. When a male tortoise finds a female, he approaches her with his neck outstretched and begins bobbing his head up and down. The scent from the gland on his chin makes him smell attractive to the female. As the male gets closer to the female, he bobs his head faster and faster. Often a female ignores him and walks away. If she does walk away, the male will follow at a short distance behind her for hours.

Eventually he catches up to the female and begins to circle around her. He gently bites her legs and shell. Sometimes he rams the female and raises her off the ground with his gular horns. When she withdraws into her shell, he climbs on top of her and they mate.

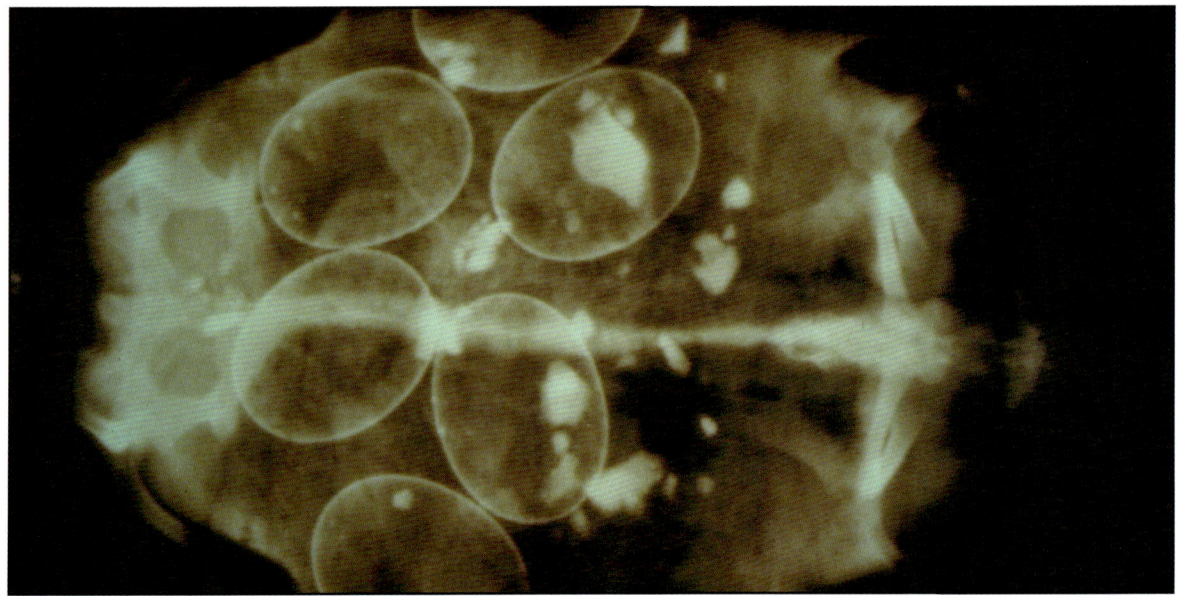

An x-ray shows eggs inside a female tortoise

TORTOISE NESTS

Sometime between May and early July, a female tortoise carefully selects a place to lay her eggs. Females often dig a nest just inside a burrow or in the apron at a burrow's entrance. Using her hind legs, she scoops out the dirt and then backs into the hole.

As if in a trance, she holds perfectly still. Soon, eggs begin to drop, one by one, from beneath her tail. She can lay from one to 14 eggs, but will probably lay between three to seven eggs. In years with little food, a female might not lay any eggs at all. When winter and summer rains bring a lot of fresh green plants, females might lay two **clutches**, or batches, of eggs.

The white eggs are nearly round and are about the size of a ping-pong ball (1-1/2 inches [3.7 centimeters] in diameter). Unlike the smooth shell of chicken eggs, tortoise eggs feel rough to the touch. The shells are hard and protect the eggs from losing water.

Tortoise eggs are eaten by predators such as badgers and kit foxes

After laying her eggs, the female uses first one hind foot, and then the other, to slowly kick a layer of dirt over the eggs. She carefully pats and presses the dirt down to conceal the location of her nest. Some females urinate on their nest and then repack the dirt. Scientists think this might repel **predators** that eat eggs.

A chunky pink-orange and black lizard, its sausage-like tail dragging behind, slowly crawls toward a tortoise's burrow. Flicking its black tongue in and out of its mouth, the lizard stops and inspects the dirt. Using its specialized tongue, the **Gila monster** smells tortoise eggs buried underground.

The Gila monster begins to dig up the eggs with its strong legs and long claws. Quickly, the female tortoise hurries to the entrance of her burrow. Charging the lizard, she nips at it and eventually chases it away. Then, she wedges herself in the opening of the burrow to protect her eggs and keep the lizard out.

Most female tortoises do not take care of their eggs. They lay them and then forget about them. Unprotected, many eggs are eaten by badgers, kit foxes and coyotes, but most tortoise nests are not found by predators.

Newly hatched tortoises have soft shells that do not completely harden until they are about five years old

Surrounded by warm earth, the eggs **incubate** underground for three to 10 months. Warmer temperatures cause the eggs to develop faster, but the eggs will not hatch if the nest becomes too hot or too cold.

In mammals and birds, whether a baby animal is a male or female does not change after the female's egg is fertilized by the male. But in most turtles and crocodiles, and in some lizards, the incubation temperature of the eggs determines whether the baby animals will be male or female. Desert tortoise eggs incubated at temperatures below 115.2° F (46.1° C) become males, and higher temperatures produce females.

The gloves on this researcher's hands help prevent disease transmission between tortoises

VULNERABLE HATCHLINGS

Some time between late August and early October, the little tortoises are ready to hatch. Inside their eggs, each tortoise uses its egg tooth to help break out of its shell. The egg tooth is a small, thorn-like point on top of each hatchling's snout that wears away in a few weeks. The little tortoises take from one to three days to hatch. Then they dig through the loose soil to the warm desert surface.

Newly hatched tortoises are tiny, about the size of a silver dollar (2-1/2 inches long [52 mm]). They look like miniature adults, except that they are rounder and lighter in color. From the moment the hatchlings crawl out of their eggs, they are on their own. The little tortoises wander off in separate directions looking for food and for shelter in lizard or rodent burrows.

Kit foxes eat small tortoises

The tiny tortoises are very fragile. Their shell is thin and soft. It feels like your fingernail because there is only a small amount of bone in the shell. Their shells do not become hard until they are between four and five years old. Until that time, they must be very careful. Unlike bigger tortoises who can hide in their hard shells, the tiny, soft tortoises are easily eaten by other animals.

The little tortoises are secretive and wary. They are difficult to see unless they are moving. If they sense danger, they either become motionless like a rock, or they scurry and hide in the shelter of bushes or rodent burrows. Many predators are attracted to movement, and if the small tortoise stops, the predators might lose interest and hunt elsewhere.

A raven's beak is strong and sharp

PROBLEMS WITH PREDATORS

A large raven, its black feathers and sharp beak shining in the sun, watches for movement in the desert. From its perch on a spiky Joshua tree, it suddenly swoops down and lands next to a baby tortoise. The tortoise freezes and then tries to dash away. The raven seizes the little tortoise. Its soft shell is easily pierced by the powerful beak of the hungry raven. Some clever ravens have learned that little tortoises are easy meals and eat as many as they can find.

Other predators also eat small tortoises. Swift roadrunners snatch unsuspecting tortoises and peck them open to eat. Snakes, such as the four-foot-long, skinny coachwhip, swallow small tortoises whole. Coyotes gobble baby tortoises in one bite. Very few hatchling tortoises survive to adulthood — only two to five out of every 100 hatchlings!

A hungry kit fox on the prowl for food is a threat to small tortoises

Even the hard shells of bigger tortoises do not always protect them from the teeth and claws of predators. Coyotes dig tortoises out of their burrows. They break into the tortoise's shell along its side and open the carapace at the top. Some tortoises, especially very big ones, are too tough for predators to eat. Many tortoise shells are scarred with toothmarks and scratches from a predator who gave up their battle with the hard shell. A frustrated coyote sometimes chews off a tortoise's leg, but a tortoise with only three legs can still survive.

It will take more than 20 years for this hatchling tortoise to grow as large as the bigger tortoise

LONG LIVES

Baby tortoises grow between 1/4 to 1/3 inch (6 to 8 mm) a year. Tortoises continue to grow for the rest of their lives but more slowly with each passing year. If they survive their first few years, the little tortoises could grow into basketball-sized adults that measure 15 inches (37.5 cm) long and weigh about 15 pounds (7 kg) (almost as heavy as two gallons of milk).

Tortoises are famous for living long lives and they even look old with their wrinkled, scaly skin. From records of tortoises in captivity and from studying wild populations, scientists know that they are among the longest-living of all animals. Wild desert tortoises live approximately 50 years.

As a tortoise grows, rings are added to each scute on its shell

As the tortoise grows, rings are added to each scute on its shell. People used to think you could tell how old a tortoise was by counting the rings on its scutes. But this method does not always work because in some drought years no rings appear while in other years with good rainfall and lots of annual plants, up to three rings are added. The shells of very old tortoises are smooth — most of their growth rings are worn away by the entering and exiting of their earthen burrows.

TORTOISES AND PEOPLE

Imagine stopping for gas in the southwest desert and getting a free tortoise! Fifty years ago it was common for gas station attendants to give or sell tortoises to customers. Even railroad workers once sold tortoises to train passengers. Travelers passing through the desert often stopped and took tortoises home to keep as pets.

The tortoise cannot easily defend itself from people

When approached by people, most wild animals run away. If caught, they bite or scratch in defense. But the slow-moving tortoise is harmless and easy to pick up. They have no fangs with which to bite, or sharp claws with which to scratch. When picked up or frightened, tortoises sometimes urinate. While this defense mechanism might cause a coyote to drop the tortoise because of the terrible taste, it does not discourage people from taking or holding them. If the tortoises cannot refill their internal canteens with rainwater, they will be unable to digest their food and might die.

In historic times, some tribes of southwest Indians ate tortoises and used their shells as tools. Tortoises were probably important in myths. Their designs are found on rocks, pottery and baskets. Mexican traders carried live tortoises on their journeys. The tortoises were sources of food and lifesaving water.

This tortoise is fitted with a radio transmitter so scientists can track its movements

HOW SCIENTISTS STUDY TORTOISES

BEEP! BEEP! The beeping sound gets louder and faster as a scientist holding an antenna approaches a tortoise with a small radio transmitter glued to the side of its shell. Tracking tortoises in miles and miles of hot desert is much easier if they can be easily located. In this way, researchers can keep track of where wild tortoises are and what is happening to them.

In order to study tortoises, scientists need to recognize each one. Some tortoises have distinguishing scars on their shells, but most look alike. Using a file, scientists notch the edge of tortoises' shells. The mark is painless and permanent and is different for each tortoise. A temporary number painted on their shells helps scientists identify the tortoises from a distance.

Tortoises make distinctive tracks

Even when scientists do not observe a tortoise they can tell if one has passed through and how recently. Just as your parents might know you are home from school when you leave your jacket and backpack in the hallway, scientists look for tortoise **signs**, such as their tracks, burrows, scats and eggshell fragments.

In the dry desert air, tortoise **scat**, or dung, can last for years. The brown scats are gradually bleached white by the sun. Scientists know that dark scats are fresh and there is probably a tortoise nearby. White scat means a tortoise was present about a year ago. Through watching tortoises, scientists learned that scats serve as territorial markers. Scat of dominant males might cause subordinate males to leave an area. (Scientists not only know what eats tortoises by watching predators in action but also from finding tortoise remains in predators' scat.)

Packrats collect a variety of objects for their nests, including scat and bones

Desert packrats collect objects to bring to their nests. Some packrats line the entrances of their nests with prickly cactus spines to keep out predators. They also carry home other appealing treasures, including tortoise shells, bones and scat. By looking in packrat nests, scientists can tell whether tortoises lived in the area. Some packrat nests, called **middens,** are thousands of years old.

With a small hand mirror, scientists focus sunlight into a bright beam and use the light to look inside dark tortoise burrows. The mirror makes a brighter light than a flashlight does and helps scientists see if a tortoise is home. Scientists also use fiber-optic scopes — the same light tubes doctors use to look inside a patient's stomach — to look into deep burrows to see if a tortoise is inside.

The desert tortoise was listed under the federal Endangered Species Act because of declining populations

A THREATENED REPTILE

At one time, this gentle reptile was a common inhabitant of the desert. But now the desert tortoise must share its home with the bright lights and glittering high-rises of rapidly growing desert cities such as Las Vegas in Nevada. Increasing numbers of people and their activities have caused desert tortoise **populations** to decline.

Desert tortoises have adapted to life in the desert and survived for thousands of years. But they are not able to adapt to the booming desert cities, which are barely a century old. The desert tortoise (*Gopherus agassizii*) is now listed as a **threatened** species under the federal **Endangered** Species Act. This Act created laws that protect the tortoises and make money available to help them survive in the wild.

As more land is covered with roads, office buildings, houses, farms, and mines, tortoises lose their homes. Their habitat becomes fragmented and the tortoises have a hard time moving from one area to another. In some areas, there are so few tortoises left that they will soon disappear.

Tortoises slowly meander across roads, unaware of the danger until it is too late. Off-road vehicles and ranchers' livestock can squash tortoises, crush their burrows, and damage the plants they need for food and shade. Some people even shoot or run over tortoises on purpose.

As development spreads farther into the desert, tortoises lose their habitat

People who collect tortoises for pets often grow tired of keeping them and release them back into the desert. Scientists think these former pets might be the source of a deadly cold-like disease, which infects and kills wild tortoises. Even though it is illegal to collect wild tortoises from the desert, some people continue to take tortoises home for pets.

Unlike the tortoise, some animals adapt well to humans and their cities. Fifty years ago, ravens were uncommon in the desert. Since more people have moved into the desert, ravens have grown more numerous. Without meaning to, people have provided the ravens with sources of food, such as garbage dumps, and more places to nest, such as powerline poles. The increasing numbers of ravens are a threat to tortoises because some ravens eat baby tortoises.

A sign cautions motorists to watch for slow-moving tortoises crossing the road

HELP FOR TORTOISES

Making a plan to save the tortoise was difficult and controversial. Once the tortoise was listed as threatened, people had to stop doing some things they had always done in the desert. Developers could not build roads, houses and schools where they wanted. Traditional desert users, such as cattle and sheep ranchers, miners, and off-road vehicle drivers, were angry.

The story of the desert tortoise shows how people with different goals and backgrounds, such as scientists and developers, worked together to save the tortoise, while still allowing human activities to go on in some parts of its habitat. This process is referred to as a Habitat Conservation Plan, which is developed by consensus of all the parties involved.

Scientists also learn about desert tortoises by studying them in captivity

Scientists studying desert tortoises learned how they are adapted to the desert. This information was used to develop a plan to save tortoises from extinction. Many steps have been taken to protect desert tortoises and their habitat. Tortoise-proof fences are put around hazards, such as along highways and around garbage dumps. Tunnels are built under highways so that tortoises can safely walk under roads without getting hit by cars. Signs remind motorists to watch out for tortoises crossing the road.

Special areas were set up where desert tortoises and other wildlife are protected. Developers of land in tortoise country are charged a fee that helps pay for the preserves and for visitor centers where people can learn about the desert. In places without good tortoise habitat, people can still construct buildings and roads, graze livestock, and drive off-road vehicles.

Special adoption programs help find qualified homes for tortoises legally removed from the desert

In the area surrounding Las Vegas, any tortoises are collected from the land before it is developed. Some of the tortoises are sent to zoos, museums and to adoption centers. People in Nevada can legally adopt these tortoises if they get a permit and can provide a good home in their backyard. In cooperation with government agencies, local tortoise and turtle club members help run the adoption program. Of course, tortoises live a long time. Can you imagine having the same pet for 50 years? Pet tortoises that need new homes can also be adopted by others.

With protection, the gentle desert tortoise will continue to survive in its natural environment

Scientists have also tried releasing some of these tortoises into other, undeveloped parts of the desert with suitable habitat. Until they dig their own burrows, the newly released tortoises are placed into artificial burrows. The new tortoises must learn where to find food and where to dig new shelters. Usually, other tortoises are already living in any good habitat. When more tortoises are added, there might not be enough food and space. Then, the tortoises might fight and some might be forced into areas where they might not survive. By studying these tortoises, scientists hope to learn how to better conduct the "translocation program."

Tortoises do not have the flair and flamboyance of bald eagles nor are they as cute and cuddly as panda bears. But their hard shells, shyness and remarkable longevity have made them a favorite of people everywhere. With people's help, the desert tortoise will be around for many thousands of more years.

GLOSSARY

adaptation: the behavior or physical features that help a plant or animal survive in its environment
aquatic: living or occurring in water
bladder: a sac that stores urine
camouflage: the coloring or appearance of an animal that helps it hide from predators or enemies
carapace: the top half of a tortoise's or turtle's hard, protective shell
clutch: a group of eggs produced and incubated at the same time
commensal: describing an animal that takes advantage of another animal, such as sharing its home, but does not harm it
drought: a long period of dry weather without rain, which can prevent plants from growing
ectotherm[ic]: an animal whose body temperature is determined by its environment
endangered: a plant or animal species in danger of dying out until it no longer exists
estivate: to be inactive because of the heat of summer
extinct: no longer living anywhere on earth; many animal and plant species have become extinct
Gila monster: one of only two poisonous lizards in the world
habitat: the area where a plant or animal normally lives
herbivore: an animal that lives by eating plants
hibernation: passing the winter in an inactive state
home range: the area in which an animal's activities occur
incubate: to hatch eggs by keeping them warm
mammals: warmblooded animals that nourish their young with milk produced by the mother's body
midden: packrat's nest where it collects and piles all kinds of debris
pallet: a shallow, dirt shelter that does not cover a tortoise's shell completely but provides protection from the desert heat
plastron: the lower half of a tortoise's hard, protective shell
population: a group of individuals of the same species
predator: an animal that lives by killing and eating other animals

prey: an animal hunted for food by other animals
range: the geographic area in which a plant or animal is found
reptile: an ectothermic animal with a backbone, scales and egg with a tough outer shell, includes lizards, snakes, turtles and crocodiles
scat: solid waste materials passed out of an animal's body
scutes: horny plates on the outer shell of tortoises or turtles
sign: anything marking the trail of an animal such as tracks and scat
species: a group of animals or plants that share similar characteristics and can breed together
terrestrial: living or occurring on land
threatened: a plant or animal species that is declining in numbers, but is not in immediate danger of extinction
wash: the dry bed of a stream